THE INVENTION
OF BUTTERFLY

THE INVENTION OF BUTTERFLY

First published in England, 2006 by Ragged Raven Press
I Lodge Farm, Snitterfield, Warwickshire CV37 0LR
email: raggedravenpress@aol.com

website: www.raggedraven.co.uk

The Invention of Butterfly
ISBN 0 9542397 9 2

Printed by Lithocraft, 35a Dane Road, Coventry, West Midlands
CV2 4JR

Christopher James

THE INVENTION
OF BUTTERFLY

Ragged Raven Press

*For Maria
and Polly*

ACKNOWLEDGEMENTS

Acknowledgements are due to the editors of the following publications in which some of these poems first appeared: *Catapult, Envoi, The Interpreter's House, iota, London Magazine, Magma, Manifold, Smiths Knoll, Staple, Other Poetry, Poetry Nottingham International, Poetry Life, Purple Patch, Reactions 2 & 3, The Rialto and South.*

Walking Southward on O'Connell Street won The Bridport Prize 2002, ***Norfolk is Heading out to Sea*** won first prize in the 20th Poetry Life Competition 2002, ***The Orange*** was a runner up in the Daily Telegraph/Arvon Poetry Competition 2002, ***Magnification*** won first prize in the Ledbury Poetry Competition 2003 and ***Import*** was long-listed for The Bridport Prize 2005.

A special thank you to The Society of Authors for an Eric Gregory Award in 2002. Thanks also to Desmond Graham and W. N. Herbert for early encouragement, Darren Giddings, Mark Smyth, James Webb, Winston Wong, Mark Tilton, Carol Tagg, Luke Heeley, Andrew & the UEA gang, Pat and Moira Weir, Bob and Janet, Tom and Doris, Billy and Hilda, Pauline and Michael, my parents, the brothers and, of course, Maria.

Cover painting:
Joseph James
The Rime of the Ancient Mariner
Acrylic and Glaze Medium on Canvas on Board 2005

*About, About, in reel and rout,
The death-fires danced at night;
The water, like a witch's oils,
Burnt green, and blue and white.*

Part II, Stanza XI
The Ancient Mariner and Other Poems
S. T. Coleridge

CONTENTS

Page

THE INVENTION
OF BUTTERFLY

*Bald eagles can actually swim. They use an overhead movement
of their wings that is very much like the butterfly stroke.*
Evolution Encyclopaedia

Anyone who keeps the ability to see beauty never grows old.
Franz Kafka

Alright, Zubin, hit it!
Frank Zappa

BANKRUPTCY AT THE SEA DRAGON AQUARIUM

The sea-horses are forlorn,
they sink like keys dropped to the bottom.
Over the years, son, it is possible they have
acquired a rudimentary understanding
of book-keeping; by now they may also suspect
that ten hour whist-drives in the back room
are not good for business.

I have taken the precaution of stationing
a *Toxodos Jaculator* by the door.
Its well aimed spit and unique gift
to judge the range of its predators
will buy me time when the sharks descend.

Halfway down the corridor
is the *Pantodon Buchholzi*,
otherwise known as the Ninja-fish.
The receivers will receive a surprise
when, as they must, they lift the lid.

I will spend my last hours here with the older fish,
like the *Meglamphodus Sweglesi*
whose anxious heart, clearly visible
through its transparent body
will not survive the shock of my departure.

The best thing you can do, son,
is take what is left in the till
and drive to your mother's.
Tell her the flotation is off, stay put
and do not open the door to anyone
and if she asks, yes,
fish would do nicely for supper.

Toxodus Jaculator: Archerfish; *Meglamphodus Sweglesi:* Red Phantom Tetra.

NORFOLK IS HEADING OUT TO SEA

It began with the twang of a telegraph wire
snapping like a banjo string above the trees.
Only the pigs heard the note of caution.
Not until bridges began to stretch like spaghetti
and an entire barn burst apart like a Christmas cracker,
did they send someone round to take a look.
There was no telling at this stage, they said,
that Norfolk was heading out to sea.

At first the trench was only a few feet across,
easily scaled in a single leap; the Royal Fusiliers
bridged the A11 with a series of steel plates
and *The Eastern Daily Press* ran the headline:
'Please mind the gap!' Hayfields parted
like the breaking of bread. Farmers reported
missing cows. Locals talked of lonely moos
from somewhere deep underground.

Soon the chasm began to fill, salt water seeping
into the breach. At night, there was a groaning,
like the shifting of tectonic plates. When a report
attributed the problem to a prolonged rain spell
and natural ebb and flow, opinion was divided.
By now, a line had been drawn, from Hunstanton
to Southwold, as if respectful of county borders.
Inevitably, there were whispers of devolution.

At the point when Swaffham was just a speck on
the horizon, the smiles began to wear thin.
Wymondham became Wymondham-on-Sea;
dry cleaners sold ice-cream. When a Minister said:
'East Anglia is breaking off like a piece of cake,'
the 8th Dragoon were sent in to retrieve Sandringham
with a series of pulleys, hooks and chains.
Plans to expand Norwich Airport, went ahead.

When it came to rest, fifteen miles offshore,
the Queen sent a message of congratulation:
'Norfolk,' she said 'is no longer heading out to sea.'
In Norwich, they were less optimistic.
The interim government issued each citizen
with a barrel of Kett's Rebellion, a life jacket,
and a copy of Collins' *Beginners' Dutch*.
On a clear day, from Thetford, you can't see much.

THE STRONGMEN OF SALZBURG

In September, in the lower countries
with the harvest in, but before ploughing begins
when the moon is more scythe than sphere,
we dance the *Schweinerne*, the boar dance,
for six straight hours, hoist dairymaids
onto our shoulders and walk from
Tyrol to Styria without breaking a sweat.
Some nights we go too far, holding up roofs
with our bare hands, or attempt the impossible
like dancing the *Schuhplattler* on one leg.
When our repertoire is exhausted on guitar
and zither, we have been known to roll boulders
from the high summer pastures to the gates
of the town, where the largest are left
as a challenge to our children's children.
We are not beyond sentimentality.
Many of us belong to closely guarded
men's societies where we compose waltzes,
and night visit songs, choose yellow tulips
or chamois feathers for our lapels
and embroider gold into our handkerchiefs.
When the womenfolk ask our business,
we show them the cattle we raise above our heads,
the reeds from the Danube in our hair
and the stone troughs we lift in our teeth.
We tell them there is strength in numbers.

REWARD

This is the first haircut of the revolution,
nothing dramatic, just a cigar and slow soak
in the salon of the *Hotel Ambos Mundos*.
Three of Fidel's lieutenants have settled in;
found they like the creak of the leather-backed
chairs, shaking out their shoulder-length hair.
They trim their *Havanas* and wait for their beards to curl.
Across their laps, sub-machine guns lie *in flagrante*
like dogs at the end of the day, grinning in their sleep.
Outside, there is the pop-weasel of rifle fire
and the thirsty roar of a blackcherry Chevrolet; but here,
there is just the suck of mousse in the palm of the hand,
the buzz of a trimmer and the clink of ice in a daiquiri.
Later, the men will take their horses to swim.

THE EXTRAORDINARY MEDITATION
OF THE SCARECROW

We picked out of the way places like Crowbeck,
or Nosterfield End, where the horizons are empty of towns
and fields fall away like the empty corners of a sloping green moon.

In summer, we stood for hours, sometimes two to a hectare,
with little more than a nod of acknowledgement
or a knowing roll of our Brussel sprout eyes.

Waist deep in the maize, we listened to the dry pant
of long distance runners as they patrolled the lanes, the tiny scamper
of the fieldmouse and the crack of buckshot in the woods.

When the clouds parted we twitched our carrot noses.
The sun burned through the holes in our straw hats
and made colanders of our heads.

We bore our crosses with ease, hung like thieves out to dry
pitched like tents, with poles slotted through our sleeves.
At dusk, the sky was a pan of mud and gold.

There was one I knew who dressed entirely in cricket whites
and stood in the corn as if he had been waved back by his captain
and just kept going; at night he waited for Mars to fall into his hands.

On quiet days, we broke our own rules and pulled faces
at the old ladies out buying goose eggs and tulips at Woodford Farm
They dropped their handbags into the honesty box.

Our loyalties lay equally with the birds and the earth
not scaring, but cautioning, marshalling the seeds above and below.
Bluetits and finches held the council of my shoulders.

When the Martians came, they burned crop-circles around us
and transported us into the silver bellies of their spacecraft.
They spat us out when they peered into our empty brains.

It is not commonly known, but we travelled,
scaling the thornbushes at night, pogoing as far as Wetheringset
and Stradbone, covering twenty miles in a single sprint.

We met old scarecrows with cracked turnip heads
and birdnest throats silenced by years of service; we glimpsed
their broken stumps in the shadows of old beeches

and stared at the remains of their plus-fours, battered trilbys
and clouded monocles; they leant up against the trees,
beckoning us on as we raced the dawn back to our own fields.

It was not lonely; we lived in a place beyond loneliness, where you can peer
into a stillness and see another; somedays we just watched barley grow;
no one can know the extraordinary meditation of the scarecrow.

WALKING SOUTHWARD ON O'CONNELL STREET

Because we do not believe,
we put our fingers in the bullet holes
in the Post Office, O'Connell Street
and watch, amazed, as the ghosts emerge
holding the brims of their flat caps.

They rest their shotguns against the wall
and smoke without fear; some share a table
with the girl with hair like Maud Gonne
in the garden of The James Joyce Centre,
amused by her laptop and pint of Guinness.

A man in a purple jacket and a bowler hat
rides through thin air on a bicycle. He waves
at the dull girl in gold spectacles who holds
four silver bullets between her fingers.
She smiles like the pages of an old book.

The unmarried women settle themselves
on the boundary of the cricket pitch at Trinity,
and distract the players with their red shoes and
semi-transparent gowns. They sing *Killarney*
and show their white faces to the sun.

Still, we are surprised, when a young man
with a blue suit and a wound to the head
asks where he can still buy snuff and a card
for his sweetheart, and why on a Monday,
he can hear an organ groaning like the dead.

THE ONLY PENNY FARTHING IN ICELAND

The only Penny Farthing in Iceland
was found in the hold of the trawlership *Silfur Tungl*
which means 'silver moon'
embedded in a hoard of herring and crushed ice.
When they hoisted it into the blue sky
it was as if it had been dipped in diamonds.

Digging deeper, they found its owner
frozen into the same bowler hat and pleasant aspect
he had chosen that morning in Liverpool,
before pedalling down to the waterfront to take in some air.
As they lowered him down his moustache cracked in two;
a boy mistook his frosted monocle for a ten krónur piece.

Reunited with his bicycle on the dockside,
the man resembled a newly commissioned statue,
still slightly bent at the knee and stiff as cardboard,
an official gift perhaps, from a neighbouring state:
their Norwegian Christmas tree or gift of *Liberty*,
a gleaming pioneer perched aloft the industrial age.

ICELAND

At night I hear, faintly, the up-gush
of muddy geysers; the distant 'pop'
of a finger expertly flicked
from inside the cheek, and the creak
of summer icebergs, drifting
a centimetre a week.

Blocking a draughty window,
there it is again, an article on
Icelandic farmers who, in bleak
winters must chip off the frozen
beards of their cattle to prevent them
from hurting each other.

And by day there is no escape either.
There is Old Icelandic to master
and sagas to digest in chilly bedrooms,
like *The Voyage Of Snedda*, who
fathered a child in every village
in the country and could eat a whole
musk-ox without ruining his appetite.

COLD STORAGE

We are currently seeking a Writer-in-Residence to spend six months
in Antarctica with the British Antarctic Survey.
Applicants must demonstrate their ability to grow a full beard
and refrain from quoting *Withnail and I* for a period
of not less than one calendar month. You will be able to rhyme
'crevasse' with 'ice-age' and make it sound convincing.
While at school, all writers must have excelled at composing
three hundred word punishment essays about the inside of a Ping-Pong ball.
The successful applicant will own their own hat and gloves.
Duties will include comparing walrus the size of chest freezers
to chest freezers, recording the gigantic copulation of the blue whale
and the dedication of a double sonnet to the setting of the midnight sun.
Poets must know at least seven words for white.
You shall not quote from Captain Oates for the duration of your stay
and may only imitate Frankie Howerd on birthdays and feast days.
These are not points for negotiation. Writers will not associate
with key personnel during working hours, nor hover outside tents
for the purpose of eavesdropping. You will however
be expected to marry smartly the worlds of art and science
even when you are so cold and depressed that you would not care
if you dropped through a fishing hole and your heart were
to stop at the shock of the water. Poets will be expected to play
the rear end of the pantomime polar bear in our annual production.
Benefits include an orange British Antarctic Survey boiler-suit,
three pairs of woollen BAS socks, a Christmas pudding for one,
and the equivalent of a pound in change for a phone call on New Year's Day.
A small toffee hammer will also be supplied for the purpose
of tapping life back into frozen knuckles. Writers may bring with them
a choice of up to three CDs, although fans of *The Smiths*
will meet with a frosty reception. Our director prefers light opera.
Before calling for an application form and further particulars, poets
are reminded that the freezing temperature of red wine is minus six degrees.
Some knowledge of Peruvian drinking songs will be considered an advantage.
Short-listed candidates will be invited to attend a selection centre
north-east of Kilbride, to test the effect of low temperature on rhyme.
They should bring two sharp pencils, a pullover and may be gone some time.

WINTER OLYMPICS

The games begin with a flame ferried
to the stove and a ring of blue stars.
The opening ceremony is a cinch:
a snip of cardboard and it's all over.
Two cups of tea and I'm ready to go.
The first event is the slalom to the shops
but from there it's downhill all the way:
a toboggan through the daytime TV,
a snowboard through a Weetabix
and a half hour float in the bath
with a wavy copy of *In Patagonia.*

Scraping frost from inside of the window
I can see I'm still in with a chance,
other curtains left undrawn across the street,
so speedskating through a recipe book,
I award myself medallions of pork
and win a podium place for my pastry
before curling up on the couch to await
your return. I awake as night falls
on the Olympic Village, draw vodka
from the deep freeze and watch
the long bottle still smoking with ice.

THE NOTE

That day was very cold.
You wore the brown corduroy hat
I had bought for you in Exeter
while waiting for my train.
You pulled it down over your eyes
as we made our way through
the cyclists and early morning joggers
in Kensington Gardens, past the folly
and the Park Keeper's Lodge
worth a million pounds.
I walk this way every day,
you said; I was astonished.
You told me I was still drunk.
I marvelled at the starved grass
at Archway where the ice-rink had been
and the water in the ornamental pond
that had frozen around the traffic cones.
They peeked out like the crimson
fingertips of the cello player
from his black fingerless gloves.
We watched him set up his music
in the subway, lightly spinning
that beautiful piece of blonde wood
on its silver stem, until he nodded,
swallowed the last of his milky coffee,
drew back his bow and pronounced a note
like the first word of the morning.

AT THE BELISHA BEACONS

On our way back to the car
in this year's new winter hats:
mine a dark, old man's flat-cap
that turns purple in the light,
yours a green corduroy dome
to replace the one you lost in Wales,
a vintage, black Volkswagen Beetle
stops for us at the crossing.
You are three months gone
with our first, and barely showing.
Our baby is not much more
than a piece of news with which
to floor our friends. It is then
I notice a photograph of the young
Frank Sinatra taped to the inside
of the back passenger window.
The driver, an elderly woman
with long, white fingers,
a sapphire coat and a brooch
in the shape of a treble clef, leans over
and winds down the window.
Frank, she insists, *you must call it Frank!*

THE FIRST WEEK

The flowers kept coming,
the marigolds, the pretty polly
until the piano disappeared
and the television became a shrine.
We primed decanters and pint glasses
with sprays of Californian poppies,
chrysanthemums and winter roses
until the trip to the back door became
an occasion of national mourning.
The banjo was buried in the corner.
We worked shifts at the sink
slicing off stems, filling jugs
and emptying the pepper sachets
of flower feed; we became experts.
Each doorbell brought a new harvest;
labels settled like butterflies
among the petals; blooms arrived
from forgotten aunts, Chief Executives,
the national rail network
and the young couple next door
we said were us five years ago.
Every day we tended two nurseries
one up, one down, until after a week
we gave up, and as the flowers waned
our baby blossomed, each first-thing smile
as new as the first buds of spring.

THE TRAVELLING PLAYER

Let those that play your clowns
speak no more than is set down for them.
William Shakespeare, *Hamlet*, Act III, Scene II

Now that I am a man,
I must walk beside the cart
checking the road for potholes and wolves

and avoid the temptation
to fill my pockets with pine-cones.
A sunflower is slotted in my belt.

There are days
when I do not recognise my own voice.
When I speak, my father speaks.

In my hand I carry an open folio,
learning my lines and cues.
In the fields, haybales are stacked ten high.

Horizons are etched on my eyes,
although my grandfather still plays the king
with the vigour of a tyrant.

My father's black hair is flecked grey
from a purgatory of pretenders and madmen.
He longs for September and the Scottish Play.

At night with the children down,
I share salt-beef and beer with the other men
and spit into the flames.

When we arrive in new towns
I rest my hand against the horse's neck
and pray we will find boys to play the women.

We pitch our tents on common ground
and excite the curiosity of the crowds with canticles,
handclaps and the crackle of a pig roast.

At the end of each day,
the sun drops like a copper penny
into the handkerchief of a cloud.

I sleep beneath the caravan,
wrapped in wreaths of long grass and dream
of the girl on the Winchester road

who, if I see again, will not resist my eye.
This time, I will show her my white teeth
and give her the flower from my belt.

If she smiles, I will lift her by her waist
and show her my strength. She will know
that I am not long to play the fool.

MAGNIFICATION

In the days when the Earth
was as young and myopic as a day old kit,
its eyes gummed with sleet and cloud

it took two alternating teams of sixteen cattle
to turn the telescope on its axis
to sweep the heavens for light;

ten kilos of sand to forge the glass;
a master optician to cast the lens
and twenty men to clear the dung.

From the domes and spires of Cracow,
they watched the lumber of glistening hides,
the glint of massive gears smeared with oil

and at its centre, Johannus Hevelius
clutching the seven yellow pages of the *Seleonographia*,
a map of the moon, his hair tied in sheaves.

For the men of science, the women brought
bowls of white *Borche* soup; for the cattlemen
they brought pounds of *Kielbasa* and jugs of good Polish beer.

Hevelius drank only small sips of *Danziger Goldwasser*,
tasting its bitterness, watching the glittering flakes of gold
settle against the palm of his hand.

He kept the straps of his sandals loose,
pushing slowly through the crowds of hooded men
knee-deep in the rank grass

his eyes uplifted toward his creation:
one hundred and forty feet of brass
gleaming like a golden finger.

It touched the sky, like the hand of Adam,
outstretched and reaching for his God,
or the claw of a circus bear, scratching at its cage.

THE CLOAK OF FEATHERS

The tailor began with the plumes of an elephant bird,
the enormous foundations, before laying on the long, golden combs
that once gave flight to the twelve-wired bird of paradise.
The lining is made from the soft down of the Mauritius pink pigeon
which tingles like low voltage electricity against the skin.
His thread was spun from the plump of the Christmas Island hawk-owl
although the delicate stitching itself is the work of a hummingbird
made possible by means of an ingenious harness that slipped over its head
and the bright blur of a needle placed in its beak.
Experts believe the heavier work to be that of the imperial woodpecker.
The long shape, it is generally agreed, resembles the form
of the great bustard, the ungainly gathering at the shoulders
and extreme delicacy about the neck being typical of the breed.
The collar is the complete set of wings from an Arctic tundra
although the white plumes which brush up against the face
are those of a swan, swiped from the Avon at midnight
by a king's assassin and sold on to buy a pair of silver pistols.
It is thought the cloak was first worn by José Morelos
a chieftain of the Mexican Revolution and on the occasion
of his execution, was removed by Salazar the priest, who himself
was arrested and visited in his cell by a flock of Jambu fruit doves.
They carried with them small pieces of white cloth, thread
and a tiny switchblade, which Salazar sewed into the lining of the cloak.
On his suicide, it changed hands, although its whereabouts
between the years 1895 and 1973 are the cause of some dispute.
Since its discovery in a tea-chest in the attic of an end-of-terrace
in the possession of an elderly English relative of Douglas Fairbanks Jr.,
it has stood here in the Hibbert chapel of Our Lady of the Rushes.
In late summer, some say, a ruffling begins among the feathers
of the migratory birds as they begin to display *Zugunruhe*,
a pining for flight; by October, the cloak has noticeably changed,
one sleeve pointing south, one north, a spectacle which draws
ornithologists, documentary film makers and curators, like those
from the Arbuthnot, who, by arrangement remove the cloak for one week
each year to clothe the skeletal mount of the dodo in the bird hall.

AT THE ALTAR OF THE GREEN GODDESS

On the polished floor of the Tate
in my torn brown cords, wet at the heel,
up close with Blake's depiction of Dante
in red robes in the third circle of hell,
an alarm bell is ringing.

A couple in blue anoraks stare at me.
Their look says: *Does this mean we have to leave?*
My look says: *Save your own skins.*
Sensing eviction, an old man carefully
re-wraps a corned beef sandwich.

A man in loafers and a worn tweed jacket
eases towards the door; his pullover has assumed
a rectangular shape and on the wall
is a gap like a missing tooth. He flashes me a smile
like a credit card swiped across a latch.

Two teachers sweep a class off the floor
in a flurry of golden cut-outs and satchel buckles;
felt-tips rattle like spent cartridges.
At the revolving doors, the anoraks pause
to drop a pound each into the donation box.

Outside, a gleaming Bentley waits in the rain.
A man with a Monaco tan has his wallet open
and is peeling off notes for his three sons poking
morosely at their tiny phones. The chauffeur
looks flustered, as the Green Goddesses round the bend.

We spill onto the wet steps and look for smoke.
Others are still inside basking in Turner's sunsets.
We cover our heads and make for the tube
while under dark skies, a young woman in a green raincoat,
gently rocking a pushchair, is bathed in violet light.

THE INVENTION OF BUTTERFLY

This new so-called stroke is nothing more than illegal lobstering.
A.A.U. swimming official

The plan was hatched in the summer of '33.
It was the reason, they said, why Coach Henry Myers,
formerly unbeaten over the one hundred free
had missed morning training every day for a week.
He was spotted instead cross-legged on the beach
at Sheepshead Bay, a green bandanna knotted tightly
over his greying hair, staring out at the waves.
When he returned, nothing was the same again.
The clouds opened like a skylight, he said, *and at once
I had it: breaststroke with no underwater recovery!*
Poolside, when we broke the huddle, we were reborn;
we grinned like insects, singled out by evolution
unfurling our wings on the turn and without breaking
a rule, devoured the competition, skimming like butterflies.

GOZZOLI'S ASSISTANTS

That summer we rose at four to the bells
of the *Torre della Rognosa*, our fingers still caked in blue glaze.
The sky was the colour of burnt sienna.

We slept six to a room, clothes and charcoals
scattered across the floor; Giotto's sketches of the *Venus*
were passed from cot to cot like a jar of wine.

Giancarlo, his favourite, dressed in the red tunic
Gozzoli gave him for his eighteenth birthday.
Our clothes we used for testing colours.

Before work, we ate oatcakes and drank goat's milk
laced with grappa, which had to be drunk quickly
before it curdled. It cured our fear of heights.

We worked mainly on the ground, gridding
and brushing in the sketches; skivvy work was all it was.
A boy could have done it.

Forty foot up, he would share his tricks with Giancarlo;
how he mixed the cinnabar with white to bring life to the saints;
how he thinly parted the lips of Saint Sebastian.

At midday they would lunch together in the *Palazzo Vecchio*,
while we chewed on our ciabatta. Imitation, we knew,
was the worst form of flattery.

When Franco and I applied the varnish
in that damp heaven of yellow ochre, we would plot our futures,
change faces; add shadowy figures at the foot of the cross.

Later, when the night smelt of cut flowers and incense,
we would doze while Brillo played his mandola,
or lob balls of mozzarella from one scaffold to the next.

It was just the shock, you understand,
when Giancarlo lost his footing high up in the dome,
tripping on a cord stretched tight over the *arricco*,

but when I saw that rockpool of blood
amongst the masonry on the marble floor,
I saw only the possibilities of colour:

the red ochre that anointed the palms of Christ
and the soft ruby of the tunic that would slip
so easily over my shoulders.

THE COLLECTOR

If you must know,
I did it for the cold, superior feel
of the leather armchair
that smells of anchovies,
pipe tobacco and cinnamon,
and which belonged to G.K.Chesterton
at the time he wrote
The Man Who Was Thursday.

I did it for the return fare
to *L'Isle de la Cite*, where, I was told,
a silver hat-pin formerly the property
of Eva Braun could be obtained
for 12,000 francs and a tot of absinthe,
in the backroom of a small haberdashery.
It was to be the centrepiece
for my ongoing collection:
'The Wives of the Dictators.'

The tariff for the nine pints
of Guinness and six whisky chasers,
it took to loosen the tongue
of the book dealer in Ballana,
I confess, was not entirely
met by my own purse.
But then, it was only he who claimed
to know the whereabouts
of the 1922 autographed edition of *Ulysses*
where, in his haste, James Joyce
had misspelled his name on the flyleaf.

I understand
you might find it disappointing
that a man of letters
be in this position
but then you are not compelled to drive
the three hundred miles
to a collectibles shop in Hexham

on the smell of the half burnt match
reputed to have started
The Great Fire of London.

It sounds like gloating,
and forgive me if that is the case,
but you have not tasted the bliss
of matching a pair of massive
Cantonese Baluster vases,
much like the ones you found
my associate and I hiding inside,
barely breathing as we clutched
in our slippery palms
the snuff bottle and handkerchief,
freshly lifted from Greenwich,
which were used to revive, briefly,
Lord Nelson at Trafalgar.
And for that you have my sympathy.

THE LITTLE ICE AGE

For five winters an old age returned,
when priests folded their hands behind their cassocks
and skated on the Thames until May.

In November we pitched our tents
and hoisted crimson standards over the estuary.
By June, only the bravest drove their stakes into the ice.

Factories froze; men made their leisurely way home,
stopping only for pots of beef tea and roasted chestnuts.
Acts of Parliament brought down the price of coal.

Each morning, mongrels with beards of frost
scrapped and slid across the ice, scattering skaters like nine-pin.
We traded sealskin at Blackfriars.

A pilot caught in a floe at Battersea traded wool and soap
until Easter, when we stripped his ship for firewood
and made tee-pees of his sail cloth.

St Paul's became an ice palace; Dominican gulls,
en route to the Arctic, roosted on the blue glass of the dome.
We prayed to crystallised saints for a thaw.

At London Zoo the doors to the giraffe house
remained closed; the elephants became darker; hairier.
They grew contemptuous of their keepers.

Veterinarians recorded among new born calves, pronounced
curvature of the tusk; polar bears stretched out on their backs
and yawned, like old actors returning to the stage.

THE COLLABORATORS

In the end it was just the two of them,
the night they stayed up all night,
drinking pint after pint of holy water.
They sank it like Czech beer - in quantity
and at length. When they ran out,
they drank Czech beer.

They spoke only to confirm their fame,
dropping words into each other's sentences
like Russian babies into sub-zero lakes.
They exchanged the typewriter like a pistol
with a spinning barrel. Outside,
the snow fell in whispers.

They told the time by the chink of the coin
in the washing machine in the next room
and listened to *The Greatest Hits of Link Wray*.
When they grew tired, they chewed their belts
and nailed a chair to the door. At three a.m.,
they began to cut their hair.

McBaird's dark ringlets fell through his fingers
as he worked. Gurney, whose hair was fair
and short to begin with, did not take long
to reach the crumbling honeycomb of his crown.
He passed the time with his impression of a man
dismounting from a Penny Farthing.

At daybreak, the door splintered open and
a tall man in a beige suit said: *It is time*.
On the table was an envelope of hair,
a broken typewriter and a note which read:
*The nakedness of woman
is the work of God.*

THE TRIP

Jimmy McDonough - Would you like to go into outer space?
Neil Young - If I knew I was going all the way. I'd like to take my family.
. . I think I could talk them into it. I'd go up on my bus.

We took to the skies in Kesey's
day-glo bus, customised for space travel
with the ghost of Neal Cassady at the wheel.

This was where it was meant to be:
in the far flung, the far out,
getting our heads together in the cosmos.

We were light years ahead of the pack.
At the last services we filled the tank to the brim,
and exchanged our road maps for star-charts.

While the attendant turned his back
we filled our pockets with Perry Como compilations
to woo our enemies in case we came under attack.

We started off smelling like roses: Ibrahim Ferrer
had stowed away in the luggage rack
with a year's supply of *Romeo y Julietta.*

I learned Cuban piano that year;
we formed a jazz quartet with Ginsberg on drums
and Tom Wolfe mugging it on bass.

We were the slight stuff:
weak chested, skinny knees, long hair
but we were tuned in all right.

Larry rigged up our sound system, the best
in the galaxy he said, although we weren't to know then
it was a deadly drain on the battery.

When the heating failed, we broke out
the Panama Red and held round-the-clock
screenings of *Five Easy Pieces*.

After the head gasket blew,
we had to close the Orson Welles season
and drew lots to look under the bonnet.

When we felt woozy we put it down
to the home-grown and plugged a hole in the skylight
with a rolled up copy of *The Village Voice*.

The WC became a lonelier place without it.
As we floated through a pinhole
in Orion's belt, we knew the game was up.

When they found us,
all the tell-tale signs were there: the expired tax disc,
the flashing fuel light and the final stage rust.

PEPYS AT SEA

I know nothing that gives a better notion of infinity and eternity than being upon the sea in a little vessel without anything in sight but yourself within the whole hemisphere.   Samuel Pepys (1683)

Rowing out alone into these exquisite doldrums
with no sound but the knock of my oars
on the edge of the boat, it is as if I am upon
a table of glass, and if I were to step overboard
the heel of my boot would clink against it.
Sea birds pass like music through the sky.
It is as quiet as a page of my diary, my palm
brushing across each entry; I have the sensation
of crossing the nave of a flooded cathedral.
The sun is a silent instrument of mathematics.
But when, Elizabeth, its light falls on the water,
like the golden hem of your petticoat, suddenly
you are with me, off the coast of Tangiers, your
eyes fixed on a horizon that belongs now only to me.

SLEIGHT

My grandfather has returned to us as a miser bird
smiting his yellow underbelly against the glass
courting his phantom mate in the window.
It is hard to think of him now as this tiny
yellow and blue spirit, lighter than a pinecone,
his bones as thin and hollow as young reeds.
He fans his wings as a desperate messenger of spring.
Still, we know it is him from the green stripe
that runs down his breast, matching his bypass scar.
Each morning, he reappears, scratching at the pane
retreating to a walnut tree when we come too close.
Our baby reaches out to him, knowing nothing
of his love of Molière, his long blue overcoat,
yellow jumper and lifelong dislike of birds.

CHRISTOPHER MARLOWE IN REVERSE

As soon as I headed south, all the signs were there:
the herd of caribou crossing the motorway bridge
making its way back to the ancient forests;
the pick-up truck abandoned on the hard shoulder
loaded with an empty crate marked *Caution: rats.*
Overhead, blackbirds thickened into slingshots
and propelled each other one by one westwards.

In the rear view mirror I glanced nervously
at the Compton typewriter from 1924 someone
had left on the back seat, which was once used
by Leonard Wolfe to type up the third chapter
of *Mrs Dalloway* and to write short but demonstrative
notes to the local pharmacist; I recited the single
line on the page: *This is the era of the blue slippers.*

I sped through the suburbs without stopping,
jumping a light as I passed Walthamstow Town Hall
which had been rented for the day by Britain's youngest
millionaire; a few doors down, the William Morris House
had been painted purple, equipped with a landing strip
and modified to fold easily in half like Tracy Island.
Warily, Anthony Trollope circled above in Thunderbird Two.

In Russell Square, I saw Dickens in his great coat
taking the flagstones two at time, gripping handfuls
of cut flowers and wet foliage for the two foot vase
at the end of his writing desk; following him home
I peered in through the window at his flickering hearth
while he sipped port, regaled his house guests and
completed on his lap the last chapter of *Oliver Twist*.

It wasn't until ten past midnight I arrived at Deptford
when the moon resembled the face of St. Stephen's clock,
the dust tracks of NASA dune buggies etching in the time.
Bleary eyed I pulled over, fed the meter and pushed open
the door to the tavern where Ingram Frizer murdered Marlowe
for the price of a bottle of wine; on the table was a dagger, a quill
and a set of Russian dolls of the Elizabethan playwrights.

As dawn broke, I found myself on the edge of old
Londinium, where I passed a cohort of Roman soldiers
clanking with boredom, stinging themselves with nettles
to keep warm and wearing helmets still stinking
of last night's soup; I gave them a wide berth as
I overtook them down the straight, and threw out
Gibbon's definitive *Decline and Fall of the Roman Empire.*

IMPORT

Shakespeare is said to have ordered his best wine from Tenerife.
                                                    Island tour guide

Still a day away but already he could taste
the cargo of bananas, almonds and Canarian wine.
It wasn't hard now to picture the ropes pulled tight
around the crates, feel their weight on his shoulder
and the word *Garachico* burnt into the wood.
For weeks he had gone without, sipped on *Grenache*
until he felt its mediocrity stick in his throat
like faint praise and flat rhyme; he had become complacent,
allowed his actors to ramble, repeated himself
and borrowed unconsciously from Marlowe.
He had turned to beer. With the Globe empty up river,
he would catch the rope himself, brush off the pine needles,
break open a case and weigh the ruby bottle in his hand
dreaming now only of his study, volcanoes and black sand.

ZIPPO IS COMING

We are Zippo's Circus' Advance Publicity Unit.
We park red noses in public places and leave
footprints a yard long in the mud-banks.
In the mornings we gather in our dressing gowns
and practise our aims by squirting the yolks
from our fried egg sandwiches.
Zippo knows when we miss our targets.
In the bakery we sprinkle sawdust in the pastries.
In the barbers there are more requests than usual
for waxed handle-bar moustaches.
We plant talking parrots in pet shops,
while the manager is looking the other way:
The birds are drilled in all our special offers.
If uptake is slow, we resort to elaborate measures.
We cast herons into the air, trailing silver banners;
we call for our Russian acrobats to patrol the treetops
and station our strong man in the thickets.
We intercept radio signals and broadcast into homes.
We are skilled in exchanging five pound notes for tickets.
At night our bill posting squad works the streets.
We do not need to bring out our dancing hippo
to let you know Zippo is coming.
We are not the last sign but the first;
we bring provincial towns to their knees,
we send word back to Zippo and Zippo is pleased.

THE WOLF GLOBAL POSITIONING SYSTEM

Saint Petroc was the younger son of the early British monarch King Glwyss. Deciding to follow a religious life Petroc went to study in Ireland and Rome, where he forecast, incorrectly, that the unseasonable rains would soon stop. In penance for presuming to predict God's weather, Petroc exiled himself to India, where he lived for seven years on an island. He returned to Britain in a silver bowl, with a wolf companion he had met in India.

There was nothing unusual about that night
adrift on the Indian Ocean, mid-May,
after the dry season but before the Monsoon
when the moon was bright as a shoal
of herring on the surface of the water.

I had established my position,
e-mailed my wife, repaired a small tear
in my Gortex jacket and had just unzipped
a small portion of my canvas roof to gaze at Polaris,
when I heard the howl of a wolf.

I listened again, but could only find
the waves lapping up against the carbon-fibre,
like fingertips brushed back and forth across a page.
I thought about that last slice of brioche I had meant
for Neptune as I passed over the Equator.

Then came the singing: a slow, lilting hymn
in what seemed like a broad Cornish accent,
but I was no stranger to the tricks of the wind.
I returned to combing the knots from my beard
and chewed slowly on some soft *chapati.*

At the point when I could pick out each word,
I could stand it no longer and tore at the roof
shouting *Sail on! I cannot be assisted!*
At first, I took it for the moon, that silver bowl,
lying deep in the water, moored alongside.

The man reminded me of a priest I knew as a boy,
sturdy, with a passing resemblance
to a bantamweight boxer; his hair was razed
to within a millimetre of dark stubble.
I come from India, he said. *God is love.*

Beside him, the wolf emerged, sitting up
on its haunches and silhouetted against the moon.
I had heard stories of such things before:
hallucinations brought on by tinned soup and loneliness.
Are you wrecked? I asked. *What is your course?*

I make for Cornwall, said the man, *where I will rid
the land of a monstrous serpent, save the life of a deer
and live as a hermit in the woods of Nanceventon.
We have three small tomatoes, a loaf and some rainwater.
My companion divines our course, I know not how.*

I threw across three packets of powdered hotpot,
my spare compass and a pair of dry socks.
I found an old chop for the wolf, which it snapped
cleanly out of the air in its terrible jaws.
For your kindness, he said, *I will give you a future.*

At once, I felt a cool breeze against my skin.
Tomorrow, he said, *the rains will begin.*
The next day I woke in a spoon of sunlight, ate a banana,
flipped open my laptop and recorded my diary entry:
Conditions - calm. A low moon last night. Nothing unusual.

THE WILD SWIMMER

We are kayaking on Bala in the rain,
suspended on the waters that run to Liverpool.
A shape, a wild swimmer, crosses our bows.

At first we think it an otter, or perhaps
a large dog, retrieving its master's stick
flung far into the centre of the lake,

until we see him retrieve an elbow
with the grace of a man replacing a new top hat.
His fingers drip with silver light.

We raise our paddles so as not to strike him,
and he flattens a hand in salute,
Awful, this weather we're having, he says.

NEWFOUNDLAND

Her eyes were a wilderness
of dark fenlands
      silver plated with rain.

Her face was the shadow
of a bird on the land.

Her skin was a prairie
of white bracken and hemlock.

She wore peacock feathers
and knew what they did not.

When they arrived,
they painted their houses
      brilliant white

and built miles of gold fencing
that stretched to the sea.

She kept to herself the secrets
of the earth,

and the language of the dark
but shared with them

the light and the light,
the sorrowful light.

AFTER THE STORM

She watches the rain,
like a cat watches the rain,
intently, completely,

examining the pine-needles
of water on the carriage window,
and out beyond

at the silver roofs of barns
and at the barrel that has
crash-landed in a field.

Her feet are pin-ball flippers,
twitching in their ankle socks,
impatient to leave.

The sky has the face of a black sheep.
Unnoticed, a tree has burst through
the lid of a machine-gun billet.

It is a week after the storm.
Trees have fainted: they lie
face down where they fell.

PROCESSION

Large, like storm drops,
catskills fall on the roof of the cortège
as we cross the avenues.

In sunlight, our Mercedes
is as black and bright as jet stone
and as sluggish as tar.

It edges by degrees,
like eyelids toward sleep,
languid as perfume and hot leather.

Outside, the city unfolds like a hand
extending its towers
and flexing its birches at the sky.

CARTHORSES

All the dead from the war
arrived at the clifftop over-reaching
the massive Atlantic.

They came in wagons like gypsy caravans,
but dull and stripped of colour,
their struts resting on the ground.

The soldiers sat facing each other
in two rows, not speaking
but not weeping either,

their hands flat on their knees
as if returning from a football match,
narrowly defeated.

The carthorses had already formed
a steady, lolloping procession
back to the battlefields.

The wagons, in their thousands,
were drawn now by ropes
into a wooden building on the cliff's edge

as large and bleak as a powerstation.
On the other side traps opened
and one by one

the carts were jettisoned into the ocean,
propelled in high, loping arcs; stragglers
leapt from the ramparts

swam deep underwater
pulled open the doors and took
their places next to their comrades.

METAMORPHOSIS

The Angel of the North is the largest sculpture in Britain and is believed to be the largest angel in the world.

It begins as a bird on a breath,
casting down from the heavens
not knowing yet

what shape it will assume,
what currents it will take
as it spirals banisters of light

until, as it glints in the sun,
it becomes a glider,
its wings as wide as a new thought.

But then we see,
they are not wings, but arms,
outstretched, munificent

and at once it is a tumbling angel,
neither God nor man,
righting itself as it falls,

and touching earth
he is as tall and graceful
as a gymnast,

presenting to the judges,
a perfectly-balanced dismount
from the stratosphere, to here.

THE ORANGE

*Santa Fina of San Giminiano spent most of her short life in prayer.
After contracting a fatal illness at the age of 10, she desperately
repented her sins (her worst lapse had apparently been to accept
an orange from a choirboy). She passed the next five years lying
on a board awaiting her death announced to her in a vision by Saint
Gregory. In the meantime, she was kept busy working miracles.*

Tim Jepson

When the stonemasons
who built this city of towers
which rise, like hands in prayer,

watched her
add rosedrops to holy water,
comb her wet black hair

and look out over sunflowers
admonished by the light,
they did not know

about her passion
for bitter chocolate,
or the orange

she accepted
from the choirboy
nor the sweet burst of its bite.

They ate their lunch
on scaffolds and swings, sang waltzes
and kept poppies in their pockets.

Although they knew
she wore only white smocks
and no shoes,

they could not tell
that, close to, her skin was
as translucent as angels' wings,

nor that as she lay upon her board,
her eyelids fluttered in sleep
with visions of Saint Gregory.

They would not have seen
the two moons in her eyes
as she watched over the dark fields

nor conceived that cardinals
might visit in secret
with their ingrowing toenails.

They laid stone upon stone,
curled their hair about their ears and
looked into the platinum eye of the sun.

No one supposed that when the bishop
shared drafts of his sermon,
her punctuation was second to none.

Not even when they saw
wallflowers spring from the towers
on the day she died

and witnessed violets bloom
from her wooden bed,
did they realise

she had blessed them
while they worked, protected them
and watched them stare;

and still they did not know
that she could never rinse the scent
of oranges from her hair.

WAYS OF SAVING MONEY

at the end of the month,
or when you have blown your last fifty pounds
on a pair of midnight blue polycotton desert pants,
include: staying in bed for a week
with a Russian novel and a pot of tea,
remembering to stock enough sugar
to taste and enough in the way of dippables.

You may watch the curtains inflate with light
but do not be tempted to part them,
although for entertainment,
you may take the occasional peek
at the man in the Versace dressing gown
who sits all day long in his conservatory,
his telephone a violin beneath his chin.

Sever your Internet connection
and challenge yourself
to a game of customised *Minesweeper*.
Promise not to leave the house
until you have successfully cleared a
minefield measuring 42 squares by 67.

Keep your PC close to the bed
and do not forget to mark your page,
for the passage about Uncle Kerenina's
trip through the snow to sell a gold watch
will be a fiend to find again.

Do not think about varying your diet
from plain digestives and peach melba yoghurt,
although on Fridays, you may eat a mini Mars bar.
Answer the phone but accept no invitations.

On payday rush to the bank,
and draw out more than enough
to treat yourself and a stranger
to a mocha with fresh cream, and a copy each
of *The Complete Works of Robert Frost*.

THE MILLSTONE

Driven to shore by falling fishing quotas
and estuary currents, I apprenticed myself
to a farmer who gave me lodgings in the loft
of a windmill, a lighthouse of the marshes.
I commanded fine views of the north fields
and the pine forests beyond, while the sails
slowly turned like each of the seasons.
In spring I ate strawberries the size of apples.
At night I listened to the applause of the rain
and considered the effect of the full moon
on the psychiatric ward in the next town.
On festivals I felt the distant boom of fireworks.
Being no trouble, the farmer soon forgot me.
I heard him shuffling among the sacks,
and watched him through the wooden slats
introduce himself to the formidable women of Mautby.
On summer nights I ventured out, visiting pubs,
passing myself off as a commercial traveller.
At midnight I made my way back along the cliff's edge
while the fireflies commemorated their dead.
When the time came, I hired a local man to help me
lug the millstone to the brow of the hill at Caister,
where we watched it thunder like a Swiss cheese
then flip like a sixpence into the sea.

RE-APPOINTING THE STONE

We started at night-fall.
Jim knew someone with a low-loader
they wouldn't miss for a couple of days
and called in a favour at the bus depot for the diesel.
The two forklifts were borrowed
from a meatpackers in Dorchester.
What goes around comes around, he said.

Down at the quarry
the gates had been left open for us.
In the foreman's office we found the
keys to the tool shed, ten rounds
of apple and pork sandwiches
and a litre of cider for every man.
Restoration, I said, is thirsty work.

Meanwhile, word had got about on site.
A hundred people had turned out in the sea-mist,
most of them in duffels and snorkels
shored up against the unseasonable weather,
but they looked ready to work.
Jim kept an eye on the archaeology students
blowing smoke rings in the shadows.

Our first setback came when Jim backed the trailer
into one of the 25 tonne sandstone uprights.
That put us back an hour at least.
But we were all team players, and when
a team of tractors took the strain
under the floodlights, there wasn't one among us
not mopping a brow in admiration.

As dawn broke, one of the cross-sarsons
dropped like a tonne of bricks onto a row of portaloos.
Initially, there was some concern for the whereabouts
of the representative from the Thomas Hardy Society
but she turned up safe and sound
in a tent with some clown from English Heritage
with a chip on his shoulder and a *Psion* organiser.

There wasn't much time to savour the moment,
when Jim gave the sign to scarper
and the police came to make their arrests,
but as Tom and I were cuffed and led away,
they took off their caps and marvelled at how
we could have put that ruin right: 5000 years
of wear and tear, undone in a single night.

THE BARN CONVERSION OWL

prefers to perch
on the roof racks of red Suzuki jeeps,

makes its nest in cast-off Prada
and flaps its wings

when the underfloor heating
is set too high.

Since its introduction to England
in the late 1980s

the Barn Conversion Owl
is rarely seen in the sky.

The Barn Conversion Owl
is often snubbed by the common owl

which prefers the darkness of tree cavities
during the hours of daylight

and breaks the necks of a dozen mice
under the cowl of night.

During the week,
the owl has the barn to itself

and spends much of its time gazing
out of the eleven-foot windows.

The Barn Conversion Owl would rather
its owners did not shop at the local Spar.

It is known to have developed a taste
for *Feta* cheese, water biscuits
         and *Pinot Noir.*

CLOSED DOORS

His front room is a mausoleum of secrets
a hundred locked safes picked up cheap at auction.
Sunday is the day for controlled explosions.
Acetylene and oxygen gas are the tools
of choice for those which defy mathematics,
pliers, and the wide handle drill.

Visitors are not permitted except by appointment.
He wears only long sleeved shirts, double buttoned
to keep the sparks from his arms and owns a canary
who lives suspended in an unlocked cage
its head cocked, listening for vibrations.
His house is miles from the nearest railway.

Some safes, he says, are tuned to a musical note
and respond better to symphonies in sympathetic keys.
He keeps a stack of vinyl next to the gramophone
and makes a little money on the side reviewing LPs.
His touch is as tender as a surgeon, pressing
the ten pence of the stethoscope to each steel chest.

He gently turns the pages of his book of combinations:
old telephone numbers and dates of birth
gleaned legitimately from the public record.
Some safes were never meant to be opened, he says;
some were meant to keep their secrets like the pyramids.
When the door springs open, I do not always like what I find.

THE MIRACLE OF THE CLOCK
(for James)

Because I am reading the diary
of an exile on Lindisfarne, because it's raining
and it's still too early to start drinking,
I talk my friends into a last minute trip
up past Alnwick and onto the island.
We buck the sleepers on the rail crossing
and leave the motorist's refuge
quivering on its whitewashed stilts,
imagining the Bible, the telephone,
the tin-opener and lifebelt inside.
The air smells of incense and seaweed.
The Ship is closed; the curtains are drawn
in our faces; already it's getting dark.
We pee in the unlit, unlovely public loos
near the affordable housing, while
an intrepid pair in Gortex hoods set off
towards the Hammer horror of the old priory.
A lone cyclist works his gears
as he snakes past the heritage centre.
Christmas trees push against
the window panes like hands; the bulbs
illuminate raindrops on the glass.
As we go to leave, one of us notices
that the clock on the dashboard
has gone back an hour; from telling
the wrong time to the right time.
On the edge of the causeway,
Cuthbert himself sees us off, disguised
as a birdwatcher with binoculars
around his neck and the head of St Oswald
held up like a lantern, guiding us
from the mudflats to the mainland.
We come to treasure our missing hour.

LEFT OF THE MOON
i.m. W.G.Wells 1919-2001

While my parents conclude your affairs,
I push open the door to the back room of your life
and find the Roman sword you won at poker
and pulled on a thief in your antique shop.
I fit my fingertips into the round, black keys
of your typewriter with *My Last Duchess*
half-copied on yellow paper curled around the reel.
Knowing some Browning, I sit down at the desk
and finger-punch as much as I can remember,
until I feel you sitting behind me, listening to
the clack of each letter as it catapults onto the page.

On the cabinet is the half bottle of brandy
you won that Saturday afternoon in summer
at my mother's school fête and drank above your shop.
It was the drink that saved you that day -
you were asleep when the American who wrote
bad cheques cleared a thousand-pounds'
of porcelain from the dealers on Elm Hill.
On the floor, by the violin case and the fractured
horsehair bow, is the hessian rucksack
you carried on your back across the desert,
the one you insisted on saving

when we cleared the shed just before your illness
and I said *It's just old*, and your eyes lit with flame.
I flick out the catch and push up the window
at the far end of the room, pour some brandy,
lean out into the night and let the crystal
refract the moon; I find the 35mm camera
you last used at my graduation, when I doffed
my mortar board and you doffed your French flat cap
as I passed out of my old life and into another.
I point it at the sky, find the emptiness in the lens
and click, until the last frame is exposed to the dark.

FIRE AT THE ICE HOUSE

It was started, they said, on the Regent's Canal
on a barge laden with bottled Guinness,
by a child tied to the roof to stop her falling in.
Like a chill, it crept up the wooden spine
of the brewery, before making the leap next door.
At the Ice House, the ice well brimmed with water
like the world's largest Scotch on the rocks.
They loaded the pure Norwegian ice onto carts,
drove it out of the yard then sold it cheap on the kerb;
common folk cupped it in their hands like quartz
bringing it to their mouths to cool their lips.
The Ice Merchant himself was last man out,
his woolly hair singed, clutching his order books,
his fur coat matted, like a cat caught in rain.

THE DOPPELGANGER

At first it was nothing more than a boot,
a brown lace-up, slightly feathered at the toe
but unmistakably mine; then a trouser leg,
pencil thin and part of a black suit I bought
for a fiver from a charity shop in Leeds.

I thought little of it, until the day
I heard a familiar voice from across a wall
and glimpsed a sheaf of blond hair
like mine, before I cropped it close.

Without thinking, I followed him
down a side street, where I found
lying face down in the gutter
the signed copy of *On the Black Hill*
I had left in a dentist's surgery two years ago.

The next morning, I found a note
in my own handwriting dropped through
my letterbox, asking me to meet him
in the Elephant Cafe, where I would
find him seated at the table beneath
the poster of Orson Welles in *The Third Man*.

I arrived early, and was sipping
a quart of plum juice when he showed up.
I was told my heart stopped for two minutes
during which time my left eye
turned slowly from green to blue:
the only thing that told us apart.

THE LONDON UNDERGROUND HAND-CART

We set off from Pimlico, just after the last train
one at each end, bowing to each other like courtiers,
railroad pioneers honouring a late night pledge.
We saluted dishevelled commuters, their ties askew
and overtook the night-buses by subterfuge.
Just for fun, we headed up the Northern Line,
inched out way past the maintenance crews,
and played out hands of whist and Chinese poker
on the long stretch between Euston and Camden Town
In the early hours we sang Portuguese drinking songs
to keep our minds off the lower back pain.
We read poems on the underground.

At three a.m. we took a wrong turn and found ourselves
at deep level, in silent tunnels where Harry Beck
appeared to us in a vision; he insisted we watch
while, like a children's party entertainer,
he fashioned a perfect version of his Tube map
in yellow, green and red live-wire insulation.
Electricity it seems, does not bother the dead.
We emerged at the abandoned platform at Aldwych
where we saw crowds of sleepy Londoners in raincoats
high collars and trilbys still waiting for their train.
At Angel, where we took turns to sleep, I dreamt
I was the steel mallet in a Swiss clock.

At Bank we didn't hang around,
consulting the manual to help us switch points,
then moved slowly beneath the Thames,
our eyes flicking upwards at the glistening roof.
It was a risk worth taking; we came up for air
at Borough Market and spent twenty pounds
on avocados, flat cider and a pair of ostrich burgers.
From there, it was plain sailing, freewheeling
along live electric rails, the mice cheering us on
just ahead of the wind and the long shadows of light.
I tore at the corners of billboards to slow us down;
we had crossed the yellow line.

When we heard rush-hour rising above us
we stopped at Gloucester Road for a bowl of sushi
and the first editions; then at Notting Hill Gate,
twenty people climbed aboard mistaking us for the first train
and stood reading their papers while they waited
to mind the closing doors; there was nothing for it,
but to make good our impression of the six fifty seven.
We're running on time, I said, *we're going out on a ledge.*
Please mind the gap between the train and the platform edge.
We burst into the open at Paddington, switched track
and made a break for the suburbs, a pint of best,
out across the fields and into the golden west.

THE LAST PRANK OF THE MARIONETTE

Might it be that this piece of wood has learned to weep and cry like a child?   C. Collodi, *The Adventures of Pinocchio*

By way of biography,
I run a one man woodshop
that produces to order,
toy boats and trains, the odd plate
and once at great difficulty and expense,
a working lighthouse for the son
of a local businessman.

I keep an oil lamp in the window
which burns steadily throughout the winter
and close early on Wednesdays.
I let my beard grow at weekends
and limit myself to a single shot
of *grappa* before bed.
From this, you will know
I am a moderate man
of moderate means.

For my keep-safes,
I have fashioned a jewellery box
from the wood of the pear tree
that grew in my grandmother's garden.
The glass false top in the lid
is perfect for keeping my notes crisp
and my enemies at bay:
a thief must face his own reflection
before breaking it open.

My first attempt I began in
pine from the Black Forest,
but it began to crack and split
and I soon threw it out into the night.
The skies were unusually dark, I remember;
behind the clouds, the moon

was barely more than the smudge
of a painter's thumb.

Some days later,
and finding myself short of wood
I retrieved it from the yard
and placed it in the fire.
It burnt with a cheerful blue flame
and a scent like new cherries.
This is not the first time I thought,
that I have gone against the grain.

Inside, there is enough space
for the silver chisel
given to me by my father,
whom I followed in the trade,
my first schoolbook
and the thin coat I retrieved
from the pawnbrokers
on the day he died.

In the warmer months,
or when I sit too close to the fire,
I am known to leak a little pear oil.
This I soak up in silk handkerchiefs,
which I send each Christmas
with a garland of plums,
and a wooden angel
to my best customer,
by which I mean my most loyal.

As winter draws in,
I am troubled by the old aches:
a certain hollowness of the heart
and a slight blackening of the feet.
My doctor attributes the unusual
enlargements of my nose
to seasonal allergies.
I tell him I agree.

At the side of the box,
there is a tiny gold handle
as delicate as an ankle,
which if wound three and a half times
will provide ten bars from *Giselle*
for the solemn twirl of the
wooden ballerina who dances with the
grace of the Fairy with Azure Hair.

And look, if you hold it up to the light,
you can see the engraving
on the underside, taken
from the crest above the stagedoor
of the Marionette Theatre,
which was lost to fire
when I was still a boy.

Now, since I am old,
and have told so much already,
I may as well confess
that if you turn the wooden leaf
at the tip of the crest, you will discover
a compartment hidden in the base
and inside a small brown packet
containing the ashes of my first feet
and the brittle corpse of a cricket.

Look further and you will see
a small silver key, which fits the lock
of the door at the end of my workshop
which you may open if you dare,
to find a lifeless puppet,
the size of a child,
slumped and staring
on a broken rocking chair.

THE SUMMER OF ERNEST HEMINGWAY

We saw him first in late May,
before the summer had really begun,
stepping out of a matinee on Drury Lane
in shorts and plimsolls and a yellow mackintosh.
He was strolling towards his touring bicycle
chained to a lamppost in Covent Garden,
sniffing pleasantly at the air; it is not everyday
that you see Ernest Hemingway gripping
a bleached-out fishing cap between his teeth
and wrestling with a combination lock.

In June, I mistook him for a postman,
staring up at a pair of pink ballet shoes
neatly crossed in the top bedroom window
of a three storey townhouse in Norwich.
He looked slightly damp and uncomfortable,
as if from a long evening on the *Nelson's Revenge*.
His beard looked a little flat; it lacked shape.
I thought I heard a soft croaking coming from
his brown leather satchel; noticed the lucky shake
of two bird-pellets of paracetamol in his hand.

Then followed the days without Hemingway,
liquid afternoons and no sightings for three weeks,
until the day in mid-July when we parked up
in a quiet church car-park at Cley, behind the butcher's
run by a look-alike, and saw him grimly dropping
his empties into the black holes of a bottle bank.
But there was no nod of recognition, no friendly hello.
Still, I knew it was him by the fact that he made no attempt
to divide his greens from his browns, and from his skin
dark as a fisherman's; his beard white as fish.

THE LEVON HELM FRESCO CYCLE

On the medieval cobbles
near the wellhead and the place
where they paraded the cow
that stood taller than a man,
we watch Odysseus pass,
come ashore to walk his hounds
and stretch his legs
in yellow three-quarter
length surf-pants.

In a sidestreet Picasso
stands in the doorway
of an antique shop wearing
a blue-striped wrestler's vest.
He sells elephant door knockers,
house-keys the size of hands
and gloomy pictures of Napoleon
in his study, awaiting arrest.
The painter squints like an oily fish.

From his back room
we hear the voice of Mario Lanza
sonorising from a gramophone.
One of us, braver than the rest,
parts the ghost-curtain of wooden beads
as if walking through a waterfall.
He sees on a shelf three jars of coins,
one marked *tobacco*, another *women*
and a third, *miscellaneous*.

Outside in the heat, I stare
up at the balcony overlooking the square
from which Grand Duke Cosimo II
announced that the plague had passed.
Just above, I make out a worn fresco cycle
showing stills from *The Last Waltz*.
Levon Helm, his head thrown back,
sings *Ophelia* at Winterland.

REDUNDANCY ON THE MASS TRANSIT RAILWAY

After seventeen years watering flowers
on the Kowloon underground
they replaced me with a sprinkler system
a microchip and an infra-red beam.
In the place where the sun slides
down the ventilation shaft like liquid gold
they exchanged my Camellias
for fake bamboo and a condom machine.
One by one, I poisoned my goldfish
and posted a letter through my neighbours' doors,
informing them of their bad habits.
With my settlement money,
I prepared a final meal of fish balls,
chicken wings and egg custard
then purchased a one way ticket
to see my great nephew in England.
I packed two dresses, my overshoes
and my smallest watering can
good for nothing but Bonsai.
For the last time, I made my way
into the Zoological and Botanical Gardens,
tearing small pieces of my identity card
and scattering them along Cotton Tree Drive
to the shopping paradise of Tsim Sha Tsui.
For keepsakes, I took Polaroids of Sim Sim
through the bars of the jaguar enclosure.
I spent elevenses in Kowloon Park,
allowing the tea to slightly burn my lips.
Finally, I rode the train to the airport
knowing each station merely by its scent.
As the plane circled over the old gardens,
the men fishing on the islands and the towers
embedded like glass splinters in the soil,
I stared at nothing but a single white cloud,
until it billowed like a white tent
pitched in a field of blue English lavender.

THE HANDWRITTEN TIMES

The history of the illuminated manuscript
did not end with Gutenberg's German psalter,
although it should have.

When the teletypewriters came clacking to a stop,
and the perforated reels sliced like tickertape,
the repairman just shrugged.

They drew lots to break the news:
if they wanted a newspaper,
they would have to write it themselves.

The editor took it on the chin. He drained the stationers
of Indian ink, harvested racks of cheap Parkers
and cleaned the shelves of Bics and rollerballs.

A calligrapher was summoned to etch the masthead.
He requested a pot of pale Chinese tea,
a silk handkerchief, a pair of ostrich feathers,

a scalpel, and half his fee up front.
Only his demand for six yellow tulips
was declined.

When word got round that a lad in the mailroom
had a legible eight point hand,
he was up at the newsdesk in minutes.

A reporter whispered at his side.
Nervous subs dictated the spellings
for the words *coppice*, *manoeuvre* and *cyanide*.

At two a.m. things looked bleak: cold compresses
were applied to wrists; dropped capitals crept in.
There was talk of doodling.

First thing, there was confusion,
then there was delight, as the first bundle dropped
from the slow moving van.

The people marvelled and paid their pence
for this minutely written, thirty-two page letter
addressed to every person in the land.

VERSOLOGY

I started out like all the rest - in the bedroom
with a couple of decks, a Hawaiian shirt, a pair of headphones
and the collected works of Wallace Stevens.
I bleached my hair, practiced my sestinas
and tried mixing Bukowski with Emily Brontë.
There were some early failures.
I trawled the sound archives, loaded up
some Frost on the ipod and remixed some Armitage.
By this time, I was playing parties for free
warming them up with a sonnet or two
before unleashing some Fenton; I put Howl on a loop
and made moonlight of their minds.
When I hit the clubs I was already a name
spinning *Past Lives Therapy* and Ezra Pound;
I played T.S.Eliot at the Ministry of Sound.
Most of them were out of it, coming up
on Gary Snyder, whispering lines
of *Migration of Birds* in the washrooms.
Girls with flushed cheeks passed me their numbers
high on Plath and with grins as wide as Hungarian clowns.
At the bar they'd barely sell a drink all night.
Afterwards, we'd meet up in midnight cafes
spark up some Muldoon and wait for the buzzing to stop.
We'd swipe the new Sweeney from each other's laptops.
By the time I played Brighton Beach
a quarter of a million showed up, calling for Ginsberg
in one voice; I fooled them with a verse of *Kaddish*
then played Ted Hughes reading from *Crow*.
The air shook like an earthquake inside a mountain.
That night the moon was like honey; the sea
as calm as Elizabeth Bishop's Club Classics Volume 3.

WORDSWORTH ON WORDSWORTH

Nobody else had noticed him,
the man at the back of the guided tour
with the Nick Drake T-shirt,
stretched as tight as a snare over his belly.
His thin, grey hair was brushed forward,
and a full set of side-whiskers
bristled like speech marks about his face.
It seemed a flimsy disguise
for a romantic poet on home-turf.

While the others peered
at the home-made candles
that burned at both ends
and which filled the room
with a thick, yellowish smoke,
and stared into the double sink
that he and Coleridge
once filled to the brim
with rum and laudanum,
he beckoned for me
to follow him into the garden.
We passed over the step
De Quincey once slipped on
during a midnight rainstorm,
shaving off an entire eyebrow
against a sharpened flint,
and settled on a bench
overlooking the lake.

Never live with your sister,
he said, pinching a thin ridge
of rolling tobacco into position.
Choose friends with habits
better than your own
and don't tinker with poems
you finished as a young man.
They will not improve.

Other Ragged Raven poetry publications:

Kung Fu Lullabies by Chris Kinsey £7.00 ISBN 0 9542397 7 6
An array of miscellaneous, very enticing poems exuding originality. A most rewarding experience to read. **New Hope International**

Seven League Stilettos by Jane Kinninmont £7.00 ISBN 0 9542397 6 8
The whole feel of the book had a spark of something that was special... pictures that could not be caught with a camera. **Reach**
Wonderfully inventive, full of vivid descriptions that are often both comic and tragic, but always surprising and magical...truly inspiring. **This Is It**

Vanishing Point by Tony Petch £6.50 ISBN 0 9542397 3 3
...throughout the book there are flashes of genius as insight combines with surprising expression. **www.suite101.com, Cold Mountain Review, U.S.A.**

People from bones by Bron Bateman and Kelly Pilgrim
£5 ISBN 0 9542397 0 9
This is a beautiful book which I very much enjoyed reading and I can recommend to anyone who loves poetry. **Jenny Hamlett, Poetry Monthly**

the cook's wedding by John Robinson £6.99 ISBN 0 9520807 8 8
I especially like the vim, the large-heartedness, the celebration of life and locality. **U. A. Fanthorpe**   *Accessible, visual and rich.* **The New Writer**

Writing on Water (anthology 2004) £5 ISBN 0 9542397 8 4
The hallmarks of the entire collection are strength, versatility, integrity and a bold fusion of highly complex emotions and rigorous intellectual questioning. **Cold Mountain Review**

Saturday Night Desperate (anthology 2003) £5 ISBN 0 9542397 2 5
A whole host of good things...emphasising the excellence of contemporary poetry today...You'll read it again and again. **Bluechrome**

The promise of rest (anthology 2002) £5 ISBN 0 9520807 9 6
One of my favourite presses, I have a Ragged Raven imprint in lounge, study and loo. **Abi Hughes-Edwards, The New Writer**

Red Hot Fiesta (anthology 2001) £6 ISBN 0 9520807 7 X
Strong, tight and characterful. **New Hope International**

Smile the weird joy (anthology 2000) £6 ISBN 0 9529897 6 1
An overflowing cornucopia of all that is best in contemporary poetry... there is delight on every page. **poetry monthly**